I take my refuge in the Buddha,
and pray that with all beings I may
understand the Great Way, whereby the
Buddha-seed may forever thrive.

I take my refuge in the Dharma,
and pray that with all beings I may enter
deeply into the sūtra-treasure, whereby
our wisdom may grow as vast as the ocean.

I take my refuge in the Saṅgha,
and pray that with all beings I may reign
in great multitudes and have nothing
to check the unimpeded progress of truth.

Avataṃsaka Sūtra

oṃ tāre tuttāre ture bhante āyuḥ puṇya jñāna puṣṭiṃ kuru svāhā

PUJA

the triratna book of buddhist devotional texts

Published by
Windhorse Publications
38 Newmarket Road
Cambridge
CB5 8DT
info@windhorsepublications.com
windhorsepublications.com

First published 1973
by the Friends of the Western Buddhist Order
First published by Windhorse Publications 1974
Sixth edition 1999
Seventh edition 2008
Reprinted 2012, 2017, 2022

Original cover design by Dhammarati
Cover design 2008 edition by Marlene Eltschig
Text layout by Hannah Davies
Printed by Bell & Bain Ltd, Glasgow

British Library Cataloguing in Publication Data:
A catalogue record for this book is available from the British Library

ISBN: 9781 899579 94 5 paperback
ISBN: 9781 899579 80 8 hardback

Contents

Illustrations & Acknowledgements

ii *White Tārā*, private collection. This form of the White Tārā mantra is chanted for the long life of our teacher, 'Bhante'

10 *Avalokiteśvara*, ITBCI School, Kalimpong

12 *Buddha*, Gandhāra, courtesy of Spink, London

23 *Prajñāpāramitā*, Java c. 1300, Museum Nasional, Jakarta

28 *Padmasambhava*, photo Brian Beresford, Nomad Pictures

30 *Vajrasattva*, block print, private collection

54 *Bodhisattva in añjali mudrā*, detail,
Dunhuang 10th century, © British Library Board.
All Rights Reserved. Shelf Number: Add.Or.5224

Every effort has been made to trace the copyright of the White Tārā and Vajrasattva illustrations. If any omissions have been made please inform the publishers so that this may be rectified in a future edition.

Translations

Translated by A.A.G. Bennett.

Selected and arranged by Sangharakshita, except *The Heart Sutra* p.24 adapted from a translation by Philip Kapleau Roshi *Prajñāpāramitā Hṛdaya Sūtra* p.53 trans. Tejananda

Publisher's Acknowledgements

Windhorse Publications wishes to gratefully acknowledge a grant from the Triratna European Chairs' Assembly Fund and the Future Dharma Fund towards the production of this book.

Triratna European Chairs Assembly

FutureDharmaFund
Transforming Self and World

Introduction

by Dhammadinna and Suvajra

Imagine a world without colour, beauty, poetry, myth, celebration, or ritual. Such a world would be a very dull, drab, dead world indeed. Such experiences are essential to human life; they cultivate our emotions, refine our senses, and enrich our imaginations. Poetry, symbol, myth, and ritual carry us – as Shelley suggests in his *Defence of Poetry* – 'to regions of light and fire, where the winged faculty of calculation dare not ever soar'. We cannot live in the realm of rational thought alone. To feel fully and vibrantly alive, we must feel in touch with all the different aspects and levels of our being.

Buddhism is a spiritual tradition, and as such speaks to us in our wholeness. Its various practices can help us to bring into being a harmony of body, speech, and mind. Throughout its history, therefore, many forms of ceremony and ritual have been developed. These range from the simplest recitation of a few verses to the most complex and lengthy rituals.

Devotional practice is multifaceted, often involving the simultaneous recitation of verses of worship, physical activity, and the conscious development of positive emotional states, as well as the mental creation of and reflection on images and symbols. Such practices clearly demand our total attention and allow no time for distraction.

Included in this book are images of various Buddhist figures. Some are depictions of the historical Buddha, others are archetypal Buddhas who do not exist on the historical level but symbolize a particular facet of the jewel of Enlightenment. The five *jinas,* or conquerors, symbolizing five sets of associated qualities of Enlightenment, are such archetypal Buddhas. Other images are of Bodhisattvas, in male or female form, who represent the inspiring principle of Enlightenment at work in the world for the welfare of the many.

All Buddhist traditions up to the present day have given a central place to ritual and devotional chanting, often in a mixture of local language and the inherited Buddhist languages, Pāli and Sanskrit. In keeping with this tradition, these practices in Triratna Buddhist Community centres around the world are also conducted in a mixture of local language and Pāli or Sanskrit. This deliberately ensures that some ceremonies which are conducted in the common, locally-shared, language (in the case of this book, English) provide an easily and readily understood focus for devotion. By chanting in Pāli or Sanskrit we are participating in a ritual that takes its inspiration from history and at the same time provides our international Buddhist movement with rituals that have a language in common. This is a strong factor in building harmony and unity.

The poetic words recited, the images invoked, and the emotions cultivated, are grounded in a coherent value system. They express our most deeply held ideals. Thus ritual practice, involving as it does the whole person, enables us to begin the task of translating our intellectual understanding into emotional experience: in other words, to transform *knowing* into *being*. They are usually performed with a number of people in a room that is focused on the beauty of a 'shrine', with its Buddha image, flowers, candles, and incense. In such an atmosphere our devotional feelings more freely find expression, enabling us to be receptive to our higher ideals and accordingly enriched.

Ritual practices within the Buddhist tradition are referred to as *pūjā,* which means 'devotional worship'. This book contains a number of such practices in the form of chants, ceremonies, and rituals, which are recited and performed at various times. For example, we may precede a period of meditation by either chanting the *Tiratana Vandanā* or reciting the *Threefold Pūjā.* Both these express devotional feelings towards the

Buddha, Dharma, and Sangha, and thus their recitation puts us in touch with our ideals, and therefore our highest and deepest motivating energies, before we meditate.

The recitation of verses is often accompanied by the making of simple offerings that symbolize both our gratitude to the Buddha for the gift of his wise example and our determination to win through to that Enlightened state. In addition to these verses, a pūjā often includes mantras. Just as Buddha and Bodhisattva statues are visual symbols of Enlightenment, so mantras are sound-symbols of Enlightenment. Some mantras consist only of sounds that are entirely symbolic, and therefore untranslatable, while others may also have some conceptual meaning. Often Sanskrit mantras such as *'oṃ maṇi padme hūṃ'* are recited. The words *maṇi padme* mean 'O, Jewel-Lotus': we can turn over in our mind the deeper and deeper implications of this. The Vajrasattva mantra, while deeply symbolical of spiritual purification, could also be considered to be more like a song, perhaps even a love song.* Whatever the form or conceptual meaning of the mantra, we are to reflect mainly on the various levels of symbolic meaning as applied to the spiritual life.

Of the various devotional ceremonies that we perform, perhaps the most spiritually important is that of the *Sevenfold Pūjā.* Traditionally the performance of this pūjā is an emotional and spiritual preparation for the arising of the *bodhicitta,* the 'will or aspiration for the Enlightenment of all beings', which is the central ideal of Mahāyāna Buddhism. Through our regular and sincere practice of pūjā, in company with our fellow aspirants, we can refine our emotional positivity to such a pitch that we begin to break through our habitual self-centredness and isolation, and

* On the conceptual meaning of the mantra, see Vessantara, *A Guide to the Deities of the Tantra*, pp.38-40.

feel an empathy with all life. In this way we prepare the ground for our own self-transcendence, which is the basis for the arising of the bodhicitta. As a result, the bodhicitta can 'arise within' or 'descend upon' the spiritual community practising together. By so practising we can bring into being what Sangharakshita has called the 'collective consciousness'. This he has described as 'a special sort of consciousness, common to, in a sense even shared by, a number of truly human individuals who follow the same spiritual disciplines and have the same spiritual ideals.' The performance of pūjā can therefore be seen as an essential element in the creation of a spiritual community.

The Sevenfold Pūjā itself consists of a series of verses, each expressing a different emotional mood. The pūjā reaches a climax in the final verse, 'Transference of Merit and Self-Surrender', in which we most vividly express our aspiration to self-transcendence.

In the first verse, 'Worship', we give expression to our appreciation of the very existence of higher values as embodied in the Buddha, Dharma, and Sangha – the 'Three Jewels'. We make offerings both mentally and in actuality, thus fully engaging our hearts and developing a mood of receptivity.

In the second verse, 'Salutation', our devotional feelings towards the Three Jewels intensify. We realize how far we still are from embodying these ideals in our lives. The respect, veneration, or even wonder, we feel as a result of such realization spontaneously moves us to pay salutation. This may be expressed physically, by bowing or prostrating, or imagined mentally.

Our worship and salutation find fulfilment in the act of 'Going for Refuge' to the Three Jewels, so in the third verse we resolve to commit ourselves to *becoming* a Buddha, *following* the Dharma, and *practising in harmony* with those whose lives are based on the quest for Enlightenment.

As we do so, we make a subtle transition from felt devotion to active commitment, and so prepare the ground for the remaining verses.

It is only when we have thus committed ourselves that we can see clearly and rationally all the obstacles that stand in our way. So in the fourth verse, 'Confession of Faults', we openly acknowledge our unskilful states of mind, the habits and tendencies that block our progress. We bring it all out into the open and, resolving not to act out of ignorance or foolishness again, try to let go of any feelings of guilt or anxiety that might otherwise inhibit our efforts.

Feeling thus unburdened, we are free to feel more deeply in touch with our own potential. The subsequent feeling of confidence and joy enables us also to see the potential in others and rejoice in their merits, in the fifth verse. Moreover, we rejoice in the existence of the Three Jewels, and in the good done by all beings everywhere. The positivity accumulated in this stage acts as the basis for our receptivity to Insight – particularly that contained in the teaching. In the sixth verse, 'Entreaty and Supplication', we admit our need for help and guidance; we ask the Buddhas and Bodhisattvas to teach the Dharma and to enlighten the darkness for all beings.

The sixth verse is often followed by the recitation of the *Heart Sūtra,* one of the most important of all Buddhist texts, which expresses the Buddhist understanding of 'conditionality' from the highest viewpoint. The recitation within the context of the pūjā is symbolic of the realization of the highest truths to which we devoted ourselves in the previous verses. The mantra at the end of the sūtra is integral to it and expresses the principle of always 'going beyond', or transcendence.

Seventh and lastly, we recite the verse of 'Transference of Merit and Self-Surrender'. This is perhaps the most beautiful verse in the whole pūjā. Here, we transfer any 'merit' we may have accrued through our practice of the pūjā towards the well-being of all.

We also express our aspiration to be of service to all beings in their search for Enlightenment and freedom from suffering. In this verse we touch on, and are perhaps rewarded with, an 'emotional glimpse' of the altruistic and other-regarding attitude that is the essential nature of the Bodhisattva.

The pūjā concludes with a set of mantras each chanted three times, and each evoking various aspects of Enlightenment. The final words, *oṃ śānti,* leave us beyond words in the peace of silence.

Perhaps we can now begin to see how important the practice of such a ritual might be for our spiritual development, and how also some uniformity of practice throughout the Triratna Buddhist Community can lead to a higher transcending unity within our Buddhist sangha. By performing pūjā we are involving ourselves in a dynamic and creative process that can radically transform us and our sangha.

Ideally, however, the performance of pūjā should not be an isolated activity engaged in only once a day. Imagine how our whole lives would be enriched if only we could experience the moods contained in the pūjā at all times! We would always feel appreciation and veneration for the ideals that we constantly express. We would continually try to find ways of expressing our commitment and try always to be scrupulously honest and open about our failings. Our lives would be full of joy and happiness as we responded to the best in people, and our hearts would be ever open to the influence of the Dharma. Finally, all our actions and practices would be imbued with the desire to benefit all beings.

If we could only practise in this way, on a moment-to-moment basis, our collective practice would take place on a much higher level: a level on which we find ourselves not only in the company of our spiritual friends, but also in the glorious company of Buddhas and Bodhisattvas.

the sevenfold pūjā

Namo buddhāya
Namo dharmāya
Namo saṅghāya
Namo nama
oṃ
āḥ
hūṃ

Worship

I

With mandārava, blue lotus, and jasmine,
With all flowers pleasing and fragrant,
And with garlands skilfully woven,
I pay honour to the princes of the Sages,
So worthy of veneration.

I envelop them in clouds of incense,
Sweet and penetrating;
I make them offerings of food, hard and soft,
And pleasing kinds of liquids to drink.

I offer them lamps, encrusted with jewels,
Festooned with golden lotus.
On the paving, sprinkled with perfume,
I scatter handfuls of beautiful flowers.

oṃ maṇi padme hūṃ

Salutation

II

As many atoms as there are
In the thousand million worlds,
So many times I make reverent salutation
To all the Buddhas of the Three Eras,
To the Saddharma,
And to the excellent Community.

I pay homage to all the shrines,
And places in which the Bodhisattvas have been.
I make profound obeisance to the Teachers,
And those to whom respectful salutation is due.

Going for Refuge

III

This very day
I go for my refuge
To the powerful protectors,
Whose purpose is to guard the universe;
The mighty conquerors who overcome suffering everywhere.

Wholeheartedly also I take my refuge
In the Dharma they have ascertained,
Which is the abode of security against the rounds of rebirth.
Likewise in the host of Bodhisattvas
I take my refuge.

The Three Refuges

Namo tassa bhagavato arahato sammāsambuddhassa
Namo tassa bhagavato arahato sammāsambuddhassa
Namo tassa bhagavato arahato sammāsambuddhassa

Buddhaṃ saraṇaṃ gacchāmi
Dhammaṃ saraṇaṃ gacchāmi
Saṅghaṃ saraṇaṃ gacchāmi

Dutiyampi buddhaṃ saraṇaṃ gacchāmi
Dutiyampi dhammaṃ saraṇaṃ gacchāmi
Dutiyampi saṅghaṃ saraṇaṃ gacchāmi

Tatiyampi buddhaṃ saraṇaṃ gacchāmi
Tatiyampi dhammaṃ saraṇaṃ gacchāmi
Tatiyampi saṅghaṃ saraṇaṃ gacchāmi

Homage to Him, the Blessed One, the Worthy One,
the Perfectly Enlightened One!

To the Buddha for refuge I go.
To the Dharma for refuge I go.
To the Saṅgha for refuge I go.

For the second time to the Buddha for refuge I go.
For the second time to the Dharma for refuge I go.
For the second time to the Saṅgha for refuge I go.

For the third time to the Buddha for refuge I go.
For the third time to the Dharma for refuge I go.
For the third time to the Saṅgha for refuge I go.

The Five Precepts

Pāṇātipātā veramaṇī-sikkhāpadaṃ samādiyāmi
Adinnādānā veramaṇī-sikkhāpadaṃ samādiyāmi
Kāmesu micchācārā veramaṇī-sikkhāpadaṃ samādiyāmi
Musāvādā veramaṇī-sikkhāpadaṃ samādiyāmi
Surāmeraya majja pamādaṭṭhānā veramaṇī-sikkhāpadaṃ samādiyāmi

Sādhu sādhu sādhu

The Positive Precepts

With deeds of loving kindness, I purify my body.
With open-handed generosity, I purify my body.
With stillness, simplicity, and contentment, I purify my body.
With truthful communication, I purify my speech.
With mindfulness clear and radiant, I purify my mind.

translation

I undertake to abstain from taking life.
I undertake to abstain from taking the not-given.
I undertake to abstain from sexual misconduct.
I undertake to abstain from false speech.
I undertake to abstain from taking intoxicants.

Dharmacāri / Dharmacāriṇī Precepts

Pāṇātipātā veramaṇī-sikkhāpadaṃ samādiyāmi
Adinnādānā veramaṇī-sikkhāpadaṃ samādiyāmi
Kāmesu micchācārā veramaṇī-sikkhāpadaṃ samādiyāmi
Musāvādā veramaṇī-sikkhāpadaṃ samādiyāmi
Pharusavācāya veramaṇī-sikkhāpadaṃ samādiyāmi
Samphappalāpā veramaṇī-sikkhāpadaṃ samādiyāmi
Pisuṇavācāya veramaṇī-sikkhāpadaṃ samādiyāmi
Abhijjhāya veramaṇī-sikkhāpadaṃ samādiyāmi
Byāpādā veramaṇī-sikkhāpadaṃ samādiyāmi
Micchādiṭṭhiyā veramaṇī-sikkhāpadaṃ samādiyāmi

Sādhu sādhu sādhu

The Positive Precepts
With deeds of loving kindness, I purify my body.
With open-handed generosity, I purify my body.
With stillness, simplicity, and contentment, I purify my body.
With truthful communication, I purify my speech.
With kindly communication, I purify my speech.
With helpful communication, I purify my speech.
With harmonious communication, I purify my speech.
Abandoning covetousness for tranquillity, I purify my mind.
Changing hatred into compassion, I purify my mind.
Transforming ignorance into wisdom, I purify my mind.

I undertake to abstain from taking life.
I undertake to abstain from taking the not-given.
I undertake to abstain from sexual misconduct.
I undertake to abstain from false speech.
I undertake to abstain from harsh speech.
I undertake to abstain from useless speech.
I undertake to abstain from slanderous speech.
I undertake to abstain from covetousness.
I undertake to abstain from animosity.
I undertake to abstain from false views.

Confession of Faults

IV

The evil that I have heaped up
Through my ignorance and foolishness –
Evil in the world of everyday experience,
As well as evil in understanding and intelligence –
All that I acknowledge to the Protectors.

Standing before them
With hands raised in reverence,
And terrified of suffering,
I pay salutations again and again.

May the Leaders receive this kindly,
Just as it is, with its many faults!
What is not good, O Protectors,
I shall not do again.

Rejoicing in Merit

V

I rejoice with delight
In the good done by all beings,
Through which they obtain rest
With the end of suffering.
May those who have suffered be happy!

I rejoice in the release of beings
From the sufferings of the rounds of existence;
I rejoice in the nature of the Bodhisattva
And the Buddha,
Who are Protectors.

I rejoice in the arising of the Will to Enlightenment,
And the Teaching:
Those Oceans that bring happiness to all beings,
And are the abode of welfare of all beings.

Entreaty and Supplication

VI

Saluting them with folded hands
I entreat the Buddhas in all the quarters:
May they make shine the lamp of the Dharma
For those wandering in the suffering of delusion!

With hands folded in reverence
I implore the conquerors desiring to enter Nirvāṇa:
May they remain here for endless ages,
So that life in this world does not grow dark.

The Heart Sūtra

The Bodhisattva of Compassion,
When he meditated deeply,
Saw the emptiness of all five skandhas
And sundered the bonds that caused him suffering.

Here then,
Form is no other than emptiness,
Emptiness no other than form.
Form is only emptiness,
Emptiness only form.

Feeling, thought, and choice,
Consciousness itself,
Are the same as this.

All things are by nature void,
They are not born or destroyed;
Nor are they stained or pure,
Nor do they wax or wane.

So, in emptiness, no form,
No feeling, thought, or choice,
Nor is there consciousness.

No eye, ear, nose, tongue, body, mind;
No colour, sound, smell, taste, touch,
Or what the mind takes hold of,
Nor even act of sensing.

No ignorance or end of it,
Nor all that comes of ignorance;
No withering, no death,
No end of them.

Nor is there pain, or cause of pain,
Or cease in pain, or noble path
To lead from pain;
Not even wisdom to attain!
Attainment too is emptiness.

So know that the Bodhisattva
Holding to nothing whatever,
But dwelling in Prajñā wisdom,
Is freed of delusive hindrance,
Rid of the fear bred by it,
And reaches clearest Nirvāṇa.

All Buddhas of past and present,
Buddhas of future time,
Using this Prajñā wisdom,
Come to full and perfect vision.

Hear then the great dhāraṇi,
The radiant peerless mantra,
The Prajñāpāramitā
Whose words allay all pain;
Hear and believe its truth!

Gate gate pāragate pārasaṃgate bodhi svāhā

Transference of Merit & Self-Surrender

VII

May the merit gained
In my acting thus
Go to the alleviation of the suffering of all beings.
My personality throughout my existences,
My possessions,
And my merit in all three ways,
I give up without regard to myself
For the benefit of all beings.

Just as the earth and other elements
Are serviceable in many ways
To the infinite number of beings
Inhabiting limitless space;
So may I become
That which maintains all beings
Situated throughout space,
So long as all have not attained
To peace.

oṃ āh hūṃ vajra guru padma siddhi hūṃ

oṃ maṇi padme hūṃ
Avalokiteśvara

oṃ a ra pa ca na dhīḥ
Mañjuśrī

oṃ vajrapāṇi hūṃ
Vajrapāṇi

oṃ tāre tuttāre ture svāhā
Tārā

oṃ amideva hrīḥ
Amitābha

oṃ muni muni mahā muni śākyamuni svāhā
Śākyamuni Buddha

oṃ āḥ hūṃ vajra guru padma siddhi hūṃ
Padmasambhava

gate gate pāragate pārasaṃgate bodhi svāhā
Prajñāpāramitā

oṃ śānti śānti śānti

Vajrasattva Mantra

(Received phonetic transcription, with Sanskrit)

OM VAJRASATTVA SAMAYA	*oṃ vajrasattva samayam*
MANUPALAYA	*anupālaya*
VAJRASATTVA TVENOPATISHTA	*vajrasattvatvenopatiṣṭha*
DRIDHO ME BHAVA	*dṛḍho me bhava*
SUTOSHYO ME BHAVA	*sutoṣyo me bhava*
SUPOSHYO ME BHAVA	*supoṣyo me bhava*
ANURAKTO ME BHAVA	*anurakto me bhava*
SARVA SIDDHIM ME PREYCHA	*sarvasiddhiṃ me prayaccha*
SARVA KARMA SUCHA ME	*sarvakarmasu ca me*
CHITTAM SHREYA KURU HUM	*cittaṃ śreyaḥ kuru hūṃ*
HA HA HA HA HO	*ha ha ha ha hoḥ*
BHAGAVAN SARVA TATHAGATA	*bhagavan sarvatathāgata-*
VAJRA MA ME MUNCHA	*vajra mā me muñca*
VAJRI BHAVA	*vajrībhava*
MAHASAMAYA SATTVA	*mahāsamayasattva*
AH HUM PHAT	*āḥ hūṃ phat*

Mantras of the Five Jinas

oṃ vajra akṣobhya hūṃ
Akṣobhya

oṃ ratnasambhava trāṃ
Ratnasambhava

oṃ amideva hrīḥ
Amitābha

oṃ amoghasiddhi āḥ hūṃ
Amoghasiddhi

oṃ vairocana hūṃ
Vairocana

The Threefold Pūjā

Opening reverence

I

We reverence the Buddha, the Perfectly Enlightened One,
the Shower of the Way.
We reverence the Dharma, the Teaching of the Buddha,
which leads from darkness to Light.
We reverence the Saṅgha, the fellowship of the Buddha's disciples,
that inspires and guides.

II

Reverence to the Three Jewels

We reverence the Buddha, and aspire to follow Him.
The Buddha was born as we are born.
What the Buddha overcame, we too can overcome;
What the Buddha attained, we too can attain.

We reverence the Dharma, and aspire to follow it
With body, speech, and mind until the end.
The Truth in all its aspects, the Path in all its stages,
We aspire to study, practise, realize.

We reverence the Saṅgha, and aspire to follow it:
The fellowship of those who tread the Way.
As, one by one, we make our own commitment,
An ever-widening circle, the Saṅgha grows.

III

Offerings to the Buddha

Reverencing the Buddha, we offer flowers:
Flowers that today are fresh and sweetly blooming,
Flowers that tomorrow are faded and fallen.
Our bodies too, like flowers, will pass away.

Reverencing the Buddha, we offer candles:
To Him, who is the Light, we offer light.
From His greater lamp a lesser lamp we light within us:
The lamp of Bodhi shining within our hearts.

Reverencing the Buddha, we offer incense:
Incense whose fragrance pervades the air.
The fragrance of the perfect life, sweeter than incense,
Spreads in all directions throughout the world.

Dedication Ceremony

We dedicate this place to the Three Jewels:
To the Buddha, the Ideal of Enlightenment to which we aspire;
To the Dharma, the Path of the Teaching which we follow;
To the Saṅgha, the spiritual fellowship with one another which we enjoy.

Here may no idle word be spoken;
Here may no unquiet thought disturb our minds.

To the observance of the Five Precepts
We dedicate this place;
To the practice of meditation
We dedicate this place;
To the development of wisdom
We dedicate this place;
To the attainment of Enlightenment
We dedicate this place.

Though in the world outside there is strife
Here may there be peace;
Though in the world outside there is hate
Here may there be love;
Though in the world outside there is grief
Here may there be joy.

Not by the chanting of the sacred Scriptures,
Not by the sprinkling of holy water,
But by our own efforts towards Enlightenment
We dedicate this place.

Around this Maṇḍala, this sacred spot,
May the lotus petals of purity open;
Around this Maṇḍala, this sacred spot,
May the vajra-wall of determination extend;
Around this Maṇḍala, this sacred spot,
May the flames that transmute Saṃsāra into Nirvāṇa arise.

Here seated, here practising,
May our mind become Buddha,
May our thought become Dharma,
May our communication with one another be Saṅgha.

For the happiness of all beings,
For the benefit of all beings,
With body, speech, and mind,
We dedicate this place.

Tiratana Vandanā

Salutation to the Three Jewels

Namo tassa bhagavato arahato sammāsambuddhassa
Namo tassa bhagavato arahato sammāsambuddhassa
Namo tassa bhagavato arahato sammāsambuddhassa

Iti'pi so bhagavā arahaṃ sammāsambuddho
vijjācaraṇasampanno sugato
lokavidū, anuttaro purisadammasārathi
satthā devamanussānaṃ
buddho bhagavā ti

Buddhaṃ jīvitapariyantaṃ saraṇaṃ gacchāmi

Ye ca Buddhā atītā ca
Ye ca Buddhā anāgatā
Paccuppannā ca ye Buddhā
Ahaṃ vandāmi sabbadā

N'atthi me saraṇaṃ aññaṃ
Buddho me saraṇaṃ varaṃ
Etena saccavajjena
Hotu me jayamaṅgalaṃ

Such indeed is He, the Richly Endowed: the Free, the Fully and Perfectly Awake, Equipped with Knowledge and Practice, the Happily Attained, Knower of the Worlds, Guide Unsurpassed of Men to be Tamed, the Teacher of Gods and Men, the Awakened One Richly Endowed.

All my life I go for Refuge to the Awakened One.

To all the Awakened of the past,
To all the Awakened yet to be,
To all the Awakened that now are,
My worship flows unceasingly.
No other refuge than the Wake,
Refuge supreme, is there for me.
Oh by the virtue of this truth,
May grace abound, and victory!

Svākkhāto bhagavatā Dhammo
sandiṭṭhiko akāliko ehipassiko
opanayiko paccattaṃ
veditabbo viññūhī ti

Dhammaṃ jīvitapariyantaṃ saraṇaṃ gacchāmi

Ye ca Dhammā atītā ca
Ye ca Dhamma anāgatā
Paccuppannā ca ye Dhammā
Ahaṃ vandāmi sabbadā

N'atthi me saraṇaṃ aññaṃ
Dhammo me saraṇaṃ varaṃ
Etena saccavajjena
Hotu me jayamaṅgalaṃ

Well communicated is the Teaching of the Richly Endowed One,
Immediately Apparent, Perennial, of the Nature
of a Personal Invitation, Progressive, to be understood
individually, by the wise.

All my life I go for Refuge to the Truth.

To all the Truth-Teachings of the past,
To all the Truth-Teachings yet to be,
To all the Truth-Teachings that now are,
My worship flows unceasingly.
No other refuge than the Truth,
Refuge supreme, is there for me.
Oh by the virtue of this truth,
May grace abound, and victory!

Supaṭipanno bhagavato sāvakasaṅgho
ujupaṭipanno bhagavato sāvakasaṅgho
ñāyapaṭipanno bhagavato sāvakasaṅgho
sāmīcipaṭipanno bhagavato sāvakasaṅgho
yadidaṃ cattāri purisayugāni
aṭṭha purisapuggalā

Esa bhagavato sāvakasaṅgho
āhuneyyo, pāhuṇeyyo, dakkhiṇeyyo
añjalikaraṇīyo anuttaraṃ
puññakkhettaṃ lokassā ti

Saṅghaṃ jīvitapariyantaṃ saraṇaṃ gacchāmi

Ye ca Saṅghā atītā ca
Ye ca Saṅghā anāgatā
Paccuppannā ca ye Saṅghā
Ahaṃ vandāmi sabbadā

N'atthi me saraṇaṃ aññaṃ
Saṅgho me saraṇaṃ varaṃ
Etena saccavajjena
Hotu me jayamaṅgalaṃ

Happily proceeding is the fellowship of the Hearers of the Richly Endowed One, uprightly proceeding ..., methodically proceeding ..., correctly proceeding..., namely, these four pairs of Individuals, these eight Persons.

This fellowship of Hearers of the Richly Endowed One is worthy of worship, worthy of hospitality, worthy of offerings, worthy of salutation with folded hands, an incomparable source of goodness to the world.

All my life I go for Refuge to the Fellowship.

To all the Fellowships that were,
To all the Fellowships to be,
To all the Fellowships that are,
My worship flows unceasingly.
No refuge but the Fellowship,
Refuge supreme, is there for me.
Oh by the virtue of this truth,
May grace abound, and victory!

from the **Jayamaṅgala Gāthā**

Blessings

Bhavatu sabbamaṅgalaṃ rakkhantu sabbadevatā
Sabbabuddhānubhāvena sadā sotthī bhavantu te

Bhavatu sabbamaṅgalaṃ rakkhantu sabbadevatā
Sabbadhammānubhāvena sadā sotthī bhavantu te

Bhavatu sabbamaṅgalaṃ rakkhantu sabbadevatā
Sabbasaṅghānubhāvena sadā sotthī bhavantu te

May all blessings be yours;
May all gods protect you.
By the power of all the Buddhas
May all happiness be yours.

May all blessings be yours;
May all gods protect you.
By the power of all Dharmas
May all happiness be yours.

May all blessings be yours;
May all gods protect you.
By the power of all the Saṅgha
May all happiness be yours.

Dhammapālaṃ Gāthā

Verses that Protect the Truth

Sabbapāpassa akaraṇaṃ,
Kusalassa upasampadā,
Sacittapariyodapanaṃ,
Etaṃ Buddhānaṃ sāsanaṃ.

Dhammaṃ care sucaritaṃ,
Na naṃ duccaritaṃ care.
Dhammacārī sukhaṃ seti
Asmiṃ loke paraṃhi ca.

Na tāvatā dhammadharo
Yāvatā bahu bhāsati.
Yo ca appaṃ pi sutvāna
Dhammaṃ kāyena passati,
Sa ve dhammadharo hoti
Yo Dhammaṃ nappamajati.

translation

Not to do evil;
To cultivate the good;
To purify the mind;
This is the Teaching of the Buddhas.

Lead a righteous life,
Not one that is corrupt.
The righteous live happily,
Both in this world and the next.

He is not versed in Dhamma who
merely speaks much. He who
hears but a little (of the Teaching) but
sees the Truth and observes it well
in deed, he is truly called
'one versed in Dhamma'.

N'atthi me saraṇaṃ aññaṃ
Buddho me saraṇaṃ varaṃ
Etena saccavajjena
Hotu me jayamaṅgalaṃ

N'atthi me saraṇaṃ aññaṃ
Dhammo me saraṇaṃ varaṃ
Etena saccavajjena
Hotu me jayamaṅgalaṃ

N'atthi me saraṇaṃ aññaṃ
Saṅgho me saraṇaṃ varaṃ
Etena saccavajjena
Hotu me jayamaṅgalaṃ

Namo Buddhāya
Namo Dhammāya
Namo Saṅghāya

Sādhu sādhu sādhu

No other refuge than the Wake,
Refuge supreme, is there for me.
Oh by the virtue of this truth,
May grace abound, and victory!

No other refuge than the Truth,
Refuge supreme, is there for me.
Oh by the virtue of this truth,
May grace abound, and victory!

No refuge but the Fellowship,
Refuge supreme, is there for me.
Oh by the virtue of this truth,
May grace abound, and victory!

Homage to the Buddha!
Homage to the Dhamma!
Homage to the Saṅgha!

Prajñāpāramitā Hṛdaya Sūtra

Oṃ namo bhagavatyai āryaprajñāpāramitāyai

Āryāvalokiteśvaro bodhisattvo gambhīrāṃ prajñāpāramitācaryāṃ caramāṇo vyavalokayati sma, pañcaskandhās tāṃś ca svabhāvaśūnyān paśyati sma.

Iha śāriputra rūpaṃ śūnyatā śūnyataiva rūpaṃ, rūpān na pṛthak śūnyatā, śūnyatāyā na pṛthag rūpaṃ. yad rūpaṃ sā śūnyatā, yā śūnyatā tad rūpaṃ. evam eva vedanāsaṃjñāsaṃskāravijñānam.

Iha śāriputra sarvadharmāḥ śūnyatālakṣaṇā anutpannā aniruddhā, amalā avimalā, anūnā aparipūrṇāḥ.

Tasmāc chāriputra śūnyatāyāṃ na rūpaṃ na vedanā na saṃjñā na saṃskārāḥ na vijñānam. na cakṣuḥśrotraghrāṇa-jihvākāyamanāṃsi. na rūpaśabdagandharasaspraṣṭavya-dharmāḥ. na cakṣurdhātur yāvan na manovijñānadhātuḥ. nāvidyā nāvidyākṣayo yāvan na jarāmaraṇaṃ na jarāmaraṇakṣayo na duḥkhasamudayanirodhamārgā na jñānaṃ na prāptir nāprāptiḥ.

Oṃ homage to the Illustrious Noble Perfection of Wisdom.

Noble Avalokiteśvara, the Bodhisattva, practising the profound way of the perfection of wisdom, observed with penetrating analysis and saw five skandhas, empty of intrinsic existence.

Regarding these [skandhas], Śāriputra: form is emptiness, emptiness itself is form; emptiness does not exist separately from form, form does not exist separately from emptiness; that which is form is emptiness; that which is emptiness is form. Likewise: feeling, determinative perception, volition, and consciousness.

In these [skandhas], Śāriputra, all phenomena (dharmas) are characterized by emptiness. They are not arisen, not ceased; not stained, not stainless; not deficient, not complete.

Therefore, Śāriputra, in emptiness, form does not exist, nor feeling, nor determinative perception, nor volition, nor consciousness. There is no eye, ear, nose, tongue, body, mind. No form, sound, smell, taste, touchable, or mental object. No eye-element, up to and including no mind-consciousness element. No ignorance, no destruction of ignorance, up to and including no old-age-and-death, no destruction of old-age-and-death. No suffering, no cause, no cessation, no path. No nondual-awareness. No attainment, no non-attainment.

Tasmāc chāriputra aprāptitvād bodhisattvo prajñāpāramitām āśritya viharaty acittāvaraṇaḥ. cittāvaraṇanāstitvād atrasto viparyāsātikrānto niṣṭhānirvāṇaprāptaḥ.

Tryadhvavyavasthitāḥ sarvabuddhāḥ prajñāpāramitām āśrityānuttarāṃ samyaksambodhim abhisambuddhāḥ.

Tasmāj jñātavyaṃ prajñāpāramitā mahāmantro mahāvidyāmantro ʼnuttaramantro ʼsamasamamantraḥ sarvaduḥkhapraśamanaḥ satyam amithyatvāt. prajñāpāramitāyām ukto mantraḥ tadyathā: gate gate pāragate pārasaṃgate bodhi svāhā.

Iti prajñāpāramitāhṛdayaṃ samāptam.

Therefore, Śāriputra, because Bodhisattvas have no attainment, they rely on the perfection of wisdom and dwell without mind-obscurations. Because their minds are without obscurations, they are unafraid. Going beyond [the four] confused views, they attain complete nirvāṇa.

All Buddhas of the three times, relying on the perfection of wisdom, are fully awakened to the utmost, perfect awakening.

Therefore, one should know the perfection of wisdom to be the great mantra, the mantra of great knowledge, the unsurpassed mantra, the most unequalled mantra, the mantra that calms all suffering; one should know it to be real because it is not false. In the perfection of wisdom, the mantra is recited thus: gate gate pāragate pārasaṃgate bodhi svāhā.

This ends the heart-essence of the perfection of wisdom.

Pronunciation Guide

In Pāli and Sanskrit every letter is pronounced and there are no diphthongs. The short vowels a, i and u, are voiced more briefly than the others which are known as long vowels. An approximate guide to pronunciation is as follows:

Vowels

a as in cut	*ā* as in cart	*ai* as in high	*au* as in out
e as in veil	*i* as in kick	*ī* as in bee	o as in low
u as in put	*ū* as in too	*ṛ* as the ri in trip	

Consonants

as in English, with the following qualifications:

g hard as in good   *c* soft as in chat

d and *t* as in English, but with the tongue tip against the back of the upper front teeth

ḍ and *ṭ* as in *d* and *t*, but with tongue tip curled up and backwards against roof of mouth

ḥ at the end of a word has a slight echo of the preceding vowel

j as in jay unless followed by *ñ* when it may be hard as in signal

ś and ṣ soft as in shin

v is pronounced somewhere between English *v* and *w*

Doubled consonants are pronounced as such, e.g. sa*dd*a as in midday, *kṣ* as in bookshop.

Nasal sounds

Before a consonant make the natural sound associated with that consonant:

ṅk as in trunk	*ṅg* as in sang	*ñc* as in crunch	*nj* as in hinge
ṇṭ or *nt*, as in tent	*ṇḍ* or *nd*, as in bend	*mp* as in limp	*mb* as in limbo

Before vowels:

ñ as ny in banyan

ṃ at the end of a word nasalizes the preceding vowel, as in the French bon.

n as in nit but with the tongue tip against the back of the upper front teeth.

ṇ as in nit, but with tongue tip curled up and backwards against the roof of the mouth.

Aspirated consonants are shown followed immediately by the letter h, and should be pronounced with an audible out-breath. Note that *th* is always pronounced as in shorthand, *ph* is always pronounced as in haphazard.

Windhorse Publications

Windhorse Publications is a Buddhist charitable company based in the UK. We place great emphasis on producing books of high quality that are accessible and relevant to those interested in Buddhism at whatever level. We are the main publisher of the works of Sangharakshita, the founder of the Triratna Buddhist Order and Community. Our books draw on the whole range of the Buddhist tradition, including translations of traditional texts, commentaries, books that make links with contemporary culture and ways of life, biographies of Buddhists, and works on meditation.

As a not-for-profit enterprise, we ensure that all surplus income is invested in new books and improved production methods, to better communicate Buddhism in the 21st century. We welcome donations to help us continue our work – to find out more, go to windhorsepublications.com.

The Windhorse is a mythical animal that flies over the earth carrying on its back three precious jewels, bringing these invaluable gifts to all humanity: the Buddha (the 'awakened one'), his teaching, and the community of all his followers.

Windhorse Publications
38 Newmarket Road
Cambridge
CB5 8DT
UK

Consortium Book Sales
& Distribution
210 American Drive
Jackson TN 38301
USA

Windhorse Books
PO Box 574
Newtown NSW 2042
Australia

info@windhorsepublications.com

The Triratna Buddhist Community

Windhorse Publications is a part of the Triratna Buddhist Community, an international movement with centres in Europe, India, North and South America and Australasia. At these centres, members of the Triratna Buddhist Order offer classes in meditation and Buddhism. Activities of the Triratna Community also include retreat centres, residential spiritual communities, ethical Right Livelihood businesses, and the Karuna Trust, a UK fundraising charity that supports social welfare projects in the slums and villages of India.

Through these and other activities, Triratna is developing a unique approach to Buddhism, not simply as a philosophy and a set of techniques, but as a creatively directed way of life for all people living in the conditions of the modern world.

If you would like more information about Triratna please visit thebuddhistcentre.com or write to:

London Buddhist Centre
51 Roman Road
London E2 0HU
UK

Aryaloka
14 Heartwood Circle
Newmarket NH 03857
USA

Sydney Buddhist Centre
24 Enmore Road
Sydney NSW 2042
Australia

sabbe sattā sukhī hontu